# MUSIC MINUS ONE CLARINET

# FIRST CHAIR CLARINET SOLOS

133
3205

## THE STUTTGART SYMPHONY ORCHESTRA
## EMIL KAHN, CONDUCTOR
## LAURENCE LIBERSON, CLARINET

*These famous clarinet excerpts from the classical repertoire are performed two times: first with the clarinet soloist on the right channel for easy removal by the at-home player. This to enable the player to study the score and listen to an interpretation by a professional performer of the highest skills. Then the orchestra performs the concerto again to accompany* **your own solo performance.**

**COMPACT DISC PAGE AND BAND INFORMATION**

MMO CD 3205

Music Minus One

# *FIRST CHAIR CLARINET SOLOS*

## *COMPLETE PERFORMANCE*

## *ORCHESTRAL ACCOMPANIMENT*

# FIRST CHAIR CLARINET SOLOS

### Beethoven Symphony No. 2 - 2nd mvt. excerpt

BEETHOVEN

**Overture from "Der Freischütz" excerpt**

Bb Clarinet

Bb Clarinet

WEBER

MOLTO VIVACE

♩ = 116

*Solo con molto passione*

Recorded excerpt starts with six bar rest.

*dolce*

music fades

**Brahms Symphony No. 3 in F - 1st mvt. excerpt**

A Clarinet

Op. 90

BRAHMS

♩. = 58

*taptap*

Recorded excerpt starts at letter A.

*mutano* in A

*mezza voce*

*p dolce*

*p grazioso*

**Bb Clarinet**

## Brahms Symphony No. 3 in F - 1st mvt. excerpt
### Op. 90

BRAHMS

**Bb Clarinet**

### 2nd movement excerpt

BRAHMS

ANDANTE ♩= 80

# March, K. 408 #1

**Bb Clarinet**

MOZART

4 taps (1 measure) precede music.

MAESTOSO ♩= 120

## "Unfinished" Symphony #8 in B minor

**Bb Clarinet**

**1st movement excerpt**

**SCHUBERT**

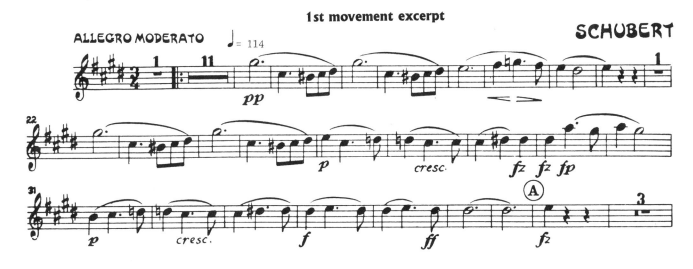

**Bb Clarinet**

**SCHUBERT**

**2nd movement excerpt**

**ANDANTE CON MOTO**

## Hebrides Overture - Fingal's Cave

### Op. 26

MENDELSSOHN

**Bb Clarinet**

## Hebrides Overture - Fingal's Cave excerpt
Op. 26

MENDELSSOHN

**A Clarinet**

## Symphony No. 5 - 1st mvt. excerpt

TSCHAIKOVSKY

MMO133
CD3205

### Excerpts from Classical Masterworks

These excerpts have been chosen with the idea of giving single instruments, principally employed in different masterworks, a chance to play their parts with the original orchestral backgrounds.

Two ideas prevail in the selection of these excerpts. One was to have the player perform only that section of a piece in which he/she is, so to speak, the soloist. Another is to provide a major section of a masterpiece in order to carry the player into the spirit of the work, even if at times he/she only doubles the melody or has an accompanying passage. Both approaches are evenly balanced in these selections.

- Emil Kahn

**Bb Clarinet**

## Symphony No. 5 - 1st mvt. excerpt

TSCHAIKOVSKY

MMO133
CD3205

MMO133
CD3205

# 3 Country Dances

**BEETHOVEN**

Beethoven used this dance as a variation in the finale of his "Eroica" Symphony.
The theme of this finale is the bass of this dance. To show this theme it is being
played by the soloist first and then the dance theme is taken up.

# MUSIC MINUS ONE COMPACT DISC CATALOG

## MUSIC MINUS ONE *PIANO* COMPACT DISCS

MMO CD 3001 Beethoven Piano Concerto No. 1 in C, Opus 15
*MMO CD 3002 Beethoven Piano Concerto No. 2 in Bb, Opus 19
MMO CD 3003 Beethoven Piano Concerto No. 3 in Cm, Opus 37
*MMO CD 3004 Beethoven Piano Concerto No. 4 in G, Opus 58
*MMO CD 3005 Beethoven Piano Concerto No. 5 in Eb, Opus 73
MMO CD 3006 Grieg Piano Concerto in A minor, Opus 16
MMO CD 3007 Rachmaninoff Piano Concerto No. 2 in C minor
*MMO CD 3008 Schumann Piano Concerto in A minor, Opus 54
*MMO CD 3009 Brahms Piano Concerto No. 1 in D minor, Opus 15
MMO CD 3010 Chopin Piano Concerto No. 1 in Em, Opus 11
*MMO CD 3011 Mendelssohn Piano Concerto No. 1 in Gm, Opus 25
MMO CD 3012 W.A. Mozart Piano Concerto No. 9 in Eb, K.271
MMO CD 3013 W.A. Mozart Piano Concerto No. 12 in A, K.414
*MMO CD 3014 W.A. Mozart Piano Concerto No. 20 in Dm, K.466
MMO CD 3015 W.A. Mozart Piano Concerto No. 23 in A, K.488
MMO CD 3016 W.A. Mozart Piano Concerto No. 24 in Cm, K.491
*MMO CD 3017 W.A. Mozart Piano Concerto No. 26 in D, 'Coronation'
*MMO CD 3018 W.A. Mozart Piano Concerto in G major, K.453
*MMO CD 3019 Liszt Piano Concerto No. 1/Weber Concertstucke
*MMO CD 3020 Liszt Piano Concerto No. 2/Hungarian Fantasia
*MMO CD 3021 J.S. Bach Piano Concerto in Fm/J.C. Bach Concerto in Eb
*MMO CD 3022 J.S. Bach Piano Concerto in D minor
MMO CD 3023 Haydn Piano Concerto in D major
*MMO CD 3024 Heart Of The Piano Concerto
*MMO CD 3025 Themes From The Great Piano Concerti
MMO CD 3026 Tschaikovsky Piano Concerto No. 1 in Bbm, Opus 23

*Available Winter 1994/Spring 1995

## MUSIC MINUS ONE *VOCALIST* COMPACT DISCS

MMO CD 4001 Schubert Lieder for High Voice
MMO CD 4002 Schubert Lieder for Low Voice
MMO CD 4003 Schubert Lieder for High Voice volume 2
MMO CD 4004 Schubert Lieder for Low Voice volume 2
MMO CD 4005 Brahms Lieder for High Voice
MMO CD 4006 Brahms Lieder for Low Voice
MMO CD 4007 Everybody's Favorite Songs for High Voice
MMO CD 4008 Everybody's Favorite Songs for Low Voice
MMO CD 4009 Everybody's Favorite Songs for High Voice volume 2
MMO CD 4010 Everybody's Favorite Songs for Low Voice volume 2
MMO CD 4011 17th/18th Century Italian Songs High Voice
MMO CD 4012 17th/18th Century Italian Songs Low Voice
MMO CD 4013 17th/18th Century Italian Songs High Voice volume 2
MMO CD 4014 17th/18th Century Italian Songs Low Voice volume 2
MMO CD 4015 Famous Soprano Arias
MMO CD 4016 Famous Mezzo-Soprano Arias
MMO CD 4017 Famous Tenor Arias
MMO CD 4018 Famous Baritone Arias
MMO CD 4019 Famous Bass Arias
MMO CD 4020 Hugo Wolf Lieder for High Voice
MMO CD 4021 Hugo Wolf Lieder for Low Voice
MMO CD 4022 Richard Strauss Lieder for High Voice
MMO CD 4023 Richard Strauss Lieder for Low Voice
MMO CD 4024 Robert Schumann Lieder for High Voice
MMO CD 4025 Robert Schumann Lieder for Low Voice
MMO CD 4026 W.A. Mozart Arias For Soprano
MMO CD 4027 Verdi Arias For Soprano
MMO CD 4028 Italian Arias For Soprano
MMO CD 4029 French Arias For Soprano
MMO CD 4030 Soprano Oratorio Arias
MMO CD 4031 Alto Oratorio Arias
MMO CD 4032 Tenor Oratorio Arias
MMO CD 4033 Bass Oratorio Arias
John Wustman, Piano Accompanist

## MUSIC MINUS ONE *VIOLIN* COMPACT DISCS

MMO CD 3100 Bruch Violin Concerto in Gm
MMO CD 3101 Mendelssohn Violin Concerto in Em
MMO CD 3102 Tschaikovsky Violin Concerto in D, Opus 35
MMO CD 3103 J.S. Bach "Double" Concerto in Dm
MMO CD 3104 J.S. Bach Violin Concerti in Am/E
MMO CD 3105 J.S. Bach Brandenburg Concerti Nos. 4 and 5
MMO CD 3106 J.S. Bach Brandenburg No. 2/Triple Concerto
MMO CD 3107 J.S. Bach Concerto in Dm
*MMO CD 3108 Brahms Violin Concerto in D, Opus 77
*MMO CD 3109 Chausson Poeme/Schubert Rondo
*MMO CD 3110 Lalo Symphonie Espagnole
MMO CD 3111 Mozart Concerto in D/Vivaldi Concerto in Am
MMO CD 3112 Mozart Violin Concerto in A, K.219
*MMO CD 3113 Wieniawski Concerto in D/Sarasate Zigeunerweisen
MMO CD 3114 Viotti Concerto No. 22 in Am
MMO CD 3115 Beethoven Two Romances/"Spring" Sonata
MMO CD 3116 St. Saëns Intro & Rondo Cap./Mozart Serenade & Adagio
*MMO CD 3117 Beethoven Violin Concerto in D major, Opus 61
MMO CD 3118 The Concertmaster Solos from Symphonic Works
MMO CD 3119 Air On A G String Favorite Encores for Orchestra
MMO CD 3120 Concert Pieces For The Serious Violinist
MMO CD 3121 Eighteenth Century Violin Music
MMO CD 3122 Violin Favorites With Orchestra Vol. 1 (Easy)
MMO CD 3123 Violin Favorites With Orchestra Vol. 2 (Moderate)
MMO CD 3124 Violin Favorites With Orchestra Vol. 3 (Mod. Diff.)
MMO CD 3125 The Three B's: Bach/Beethoven/Brahms
MMO CD 3126 Vivaldi Concerti in Am, D, Am Opus 3 No. 6,9,8
MMO CD 3127 Vivaldi "The Four Seasons" 2 CD set $29.98 each
MMO CD 3128 Vivaldi "La Tempesta di Mare" Opus 8 No. 5
　　　　　　　Albinoni: Violin Concerto in A
MMO CD 3129 Vivaldi: Violin Concerto Opus 3 No. 12
　　　　　　　Vivaldi Violin Concerto Opus 8, No. 6 "Il Piacere"

*Available by Summer 1994

## MUSIC MINUS ONE *FLUTE* COMPACT DISCS

MMO CD 3300 Mozart Concerto in D/Quantz Concerto in G
MMO CD 3301 Mozart Flute Concerto in G major
MMO CD 3302 J.S. Bach Suite No. 2 in Bm
MMO CD 3303 Boccherini/Vivaldi Concerti/Mozart Andante
MMO CD 3304 Haydn/Vivaldi/Frederick "The Great" Concerti
MMO CD 3305 Vivaldi/Telemann/Leclair Flute Concerti
MMO CD 3306 J.S. Bach Brandenburg No. 2/Haydn Concerto
MMO CD 3307 J.S. Bach Triple Concerto/Vivaldi Concerto No. 9
*MMO CD 3308 Mozart/Stamitz Flute Quartets
*MMO CD 3309 Haydn London Trios
*MMO CD 3310 J.S. Bach Brandenburg Concerti No. 4 and No. 5
*MMO CD 3311 W.A. Mozart Three Flute Quartets
*MMO CD 3312 Telemann Am Suite/Gluck 'Orpheus' Scene/Pergolesi Conc. in G
*MMO CD 3313 Flute Song Easy familiar Classics
MMO CD 3314 Vivaldi 3 Flute Concerti RV 427, 438, Opus 10 No. 5
MMO CD 3315 Vivaldi 3 Flute Concerti RV 440, Opus 10 No. 4, RV 429

*Available by Fall 1994

## MUSIC MINUS ONE *OBOE* COMPACT DISCS

MMO CD 3400 Albinoni Three Oboe Concerti Opus 7 No. 3, No. 6, Opus 9 No. 2

# MUSIC MINUS ONE
50 Executive Boulevard
Elmsford, New York 10523-1325
Phone: 914-592-1188
Fax: 914-592-3116